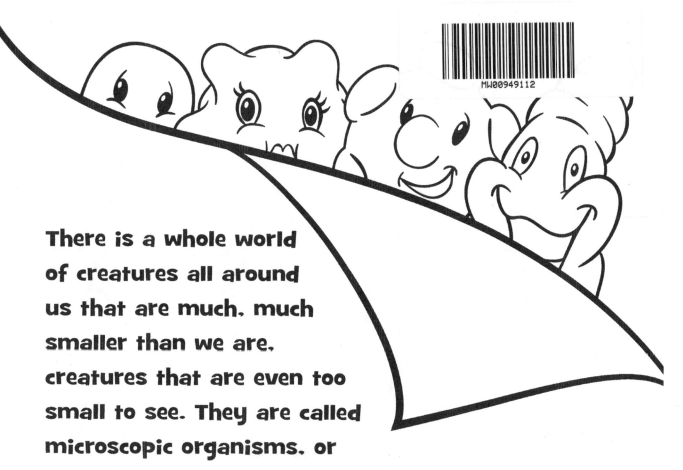

There is a whole world of creatures all around us that are much, much smaller than we are, creatures that are even too small to see. They are called microscopic organisms, or microbes! Most of them live in the water or soil, minding their own little business. We hardly know that they're there (unless we peek at them through a microscope). Some do magical things for us: like little fairies, they make bread and yogurt, or work to help us stay healthy. Others wander inside our bodies and cause trouble by making us sneeze, or feel tired or sick. In this book, you will be introduced to some of the tiny creatures that share our world with us. Have fun getting to know them!

Wash your hands for at least 15 seconds before eating — and after coughing, sneezing, or wiping your nose!

There are more than **250** different kinds of cold viruses

One sneeze sends tens of thousands of droplets filled with germs 20 feet or more through the air!

Some germs that make you sick don't like too much heat. When you get a temperature, your body is getting hot to make these germs go away!

The word "flu" is short for influenza, back when the stars were thought to "influence" the start of an epidemic.

Germs can live on many surfaces such as sinks or countertops. Keeping your house clean helps to stop germs from spreading.

Honey and warm tea can help your throat feel better if it's sore.

A throat culture can determine if a sore throat is viral or bacterial — only bacteria respond to antibiotics.

But if your throat really hurts, a doctor can look and see if something is wrong.

Gas. air. or even spicy foods can make your stomach ache.

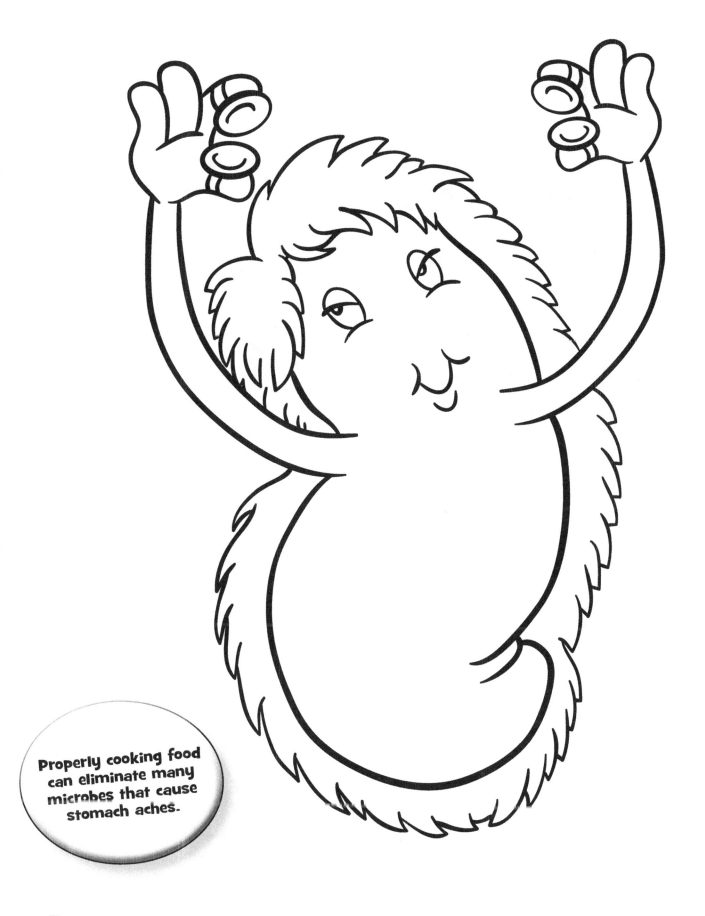

Properly cooking food can eliminate many microbes that cause stomach aches.

But so can too many microbes playing in your stomach!

Everyone loves kisses!

Epstein-Barr virus can cause the spleen to be enlarged: rough sports should be avoided.

**But be careful: if you share food and drink,
you might also share germs!**

Spicy foods and onions have a lot of sulfur in them
that microbes like to eat.

Bad breath bacteria produce hydrogen sulfide. the same chemical found in rotting eggs.

But when microbes eat sulfur. they make a gas that smells bad.

**Microbes hide on your teeth,
looking for little crumbs of food to eat.**

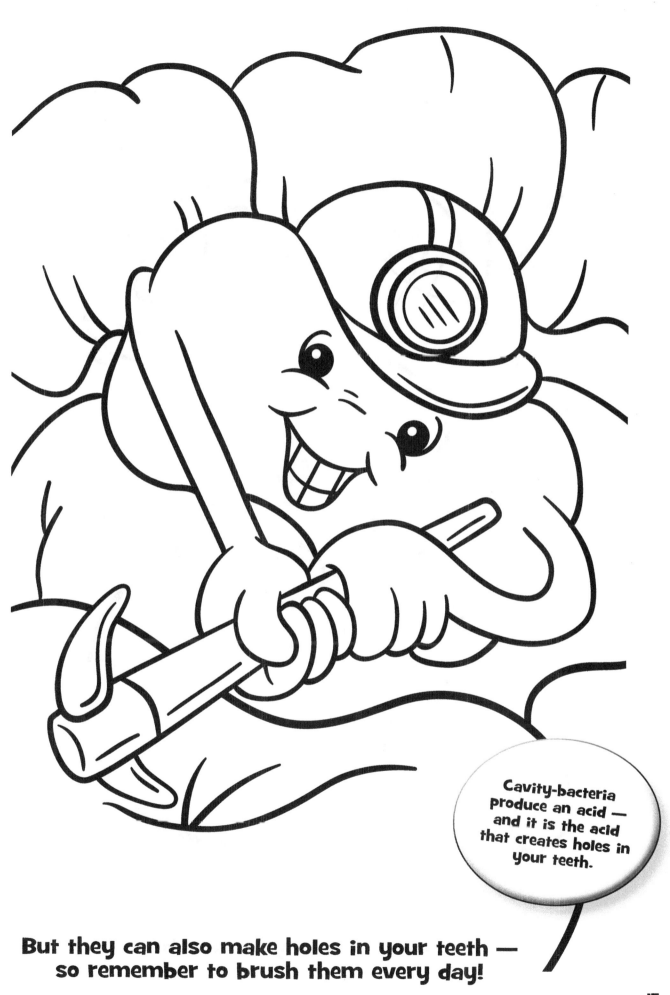

Cavity-bacteria produce an acid — and it is the acid that creates holes in your teeth.

But they can also make holes in your teeth — so remember to brush them every day!

Loud noises can make your ears hurt.

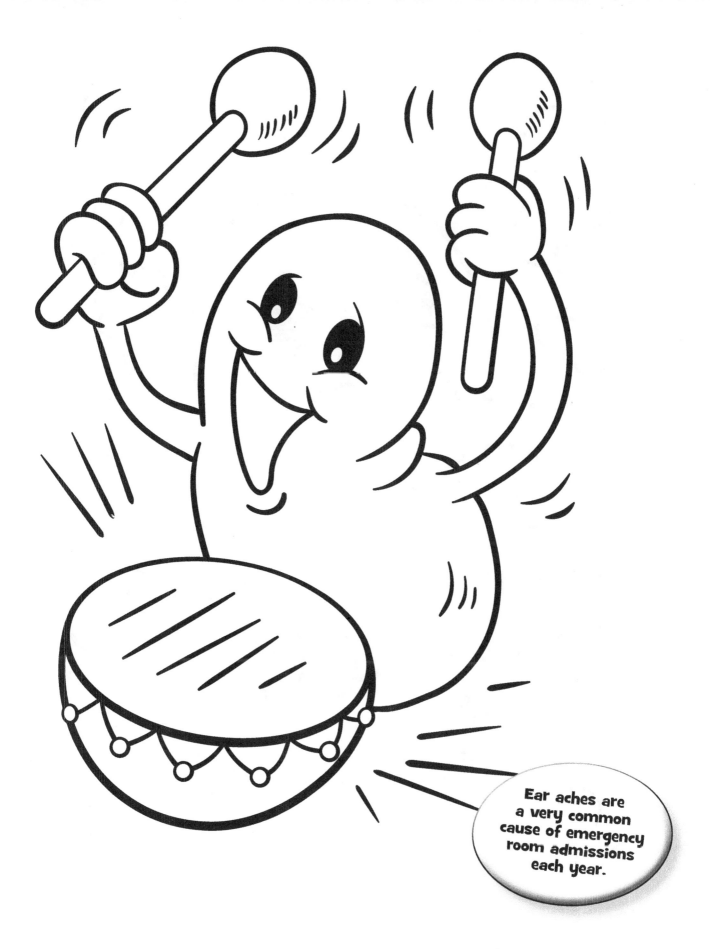

But some germs can cause an infection which can make your ear sore.

Breathing dust or smoke or even cold air can make you cough.

But if you have too many microbes in your lungs,
they can make you cough too.

Penicillin is a tiny microbe that grows on many types of cheeses!

21

**Bifido lives in your stomach.
It is a good microbe that helps you digest food.**

**It is called Bi-fido because it has two necks
(just like a bi-cycle has two wheels!)**

Yeast is an amazing microbe which can make bread.

As yeast digests the sugar in the bread, they release carbon-dioxide bubbles, like the ones found in carbonated beverages.

When it eats sugar, it blows bubbles into the warm dough and it makes it rise!

Yogurt is made by special microbes that can turn milk into a food.

Many people like to eat yogurt, too! Do you?

Millions of tiny creatures live in the seas and oceans.

Paramecium is one of the model organisms that students study in school.

Tiny creatures also live in puddles — and even in tiny drops of water! They are much smaller than fish.

Many microscopic creatures can ooze around and change shapes.

The word amoeba comes from the greek word "to change!"

An amoeba can make lots of shapes!